A THEOLOGY OF DESIRE

Meditations on intimacy, consummation, and the longing of God

A THEOLOGY OF DESIRE

*Meditations on intimacy, consummation, and
the longing of God*

SUZANNE DEWITT HALL

DH Strategies

First Edition

ISBN-13: 978-0-9864080-8-3

Printed in the United States of America

DEDICATION

I met my Beloved while in the depths of several kinds of heartache. Our friendship developed over two Christmases, dozens of Bible studies, and numerous shared prayers. As our friendship deepened, we took turns offering hidden parts of ourselves in order to measure the other's trustworthiness. All this took place before our relationship pivoted, shifting the axis of our universes by transforming from friendship to love.

My action of trust was to share a blog I'd been writing for some years. It wasn't a secret, but no one was reading it. I used it as a place to capture thought and explore ideas related to my deepest pain and longing. I handed her the blog address as if it were a delicate object, spun from threads of glass. It was my heart, really, connected to my soul, and it centered on a deep vulnerability. The writing revealed secrets written in plain sight. She told me later that she'd stayed up into the night reading it, sometimes crying. She told me later that it was beautiful. She told me later that I needed to be read.

The blog was called *A Theology of Desire*. While my understanding of God has shifted significantly since the years in which I wrote it, the roots of this devotional are in that space, along with many of its thoughts and quotes. If Dolce had not walked into my life, this book wouldn't exist today.

When we met, we had no idea that our eternities were connected. When we tested trust, we had no idea how much we would come to rely on each other. In this and in so many other things, I have proof of a very loving God.

Thank you, sweet Dolce. I love you, all ways.

CONTENTS

KNOW ME MORE

Share a peach with me
Softly ripe
And by it
Know me more.

INTRODUCTION

As I explored the deep longings of my heart and captured them in my *A Theology of Desire* blog, I came to realize that the essence of divinity is an intense yearning for unity. It's taken a long time to transform these thoughts into a book, but that's what you're holding now.

My prayer is that in opening your heart and mind to the words captured here, you'll understand God more tangibly, mystically, and experientially. This goes for whether you are part of a married couple, a sexually active single person, or celibate. Desire and longing are part of the human condition, regardless of the kind of relationship each person is in, or not in.

And desire is an experience of God.

I'm not inventing anything new in this book. I'm exploring ideas that are as old as the Christian faith itself, and even older. The lines of thought cut across denominational lines and concept barriers which tend to create distance between Christians.

So come along with me and with the souls of wise Christians from years past, on a journey of exploration into intimacy, consummation, and the desire of, and for, God.

GOD'S PRONOUNS

Christians proclaim a Trinity of three persons in one God, male and female as explained in the Genesis creation accounts. You will therefore find the following pronouns used throughout the book:

Creator/Father They/Them/Theirs

Jesus He/Him/His

Holy Spirit She/Her/Hers

GUIDE TO BIBLE TRANSLATIONS

A variety of Bible translations are used throughout this devotional. Acronyms for included versions are listed below.

ASV	American Standard Version
DARBY	Darby Translation
DRA	Douay-Rheims 1899 American Edition
KJV	King James Version
WEB	World English Bible
YLT	Young's Literal Translation

How to Use This Book

Devotional entries are short, and this topic is compelling. You might be tempted to keep reading after the first day, potentially even consuming the whole book in a single sitting. While you can of course do that, I hope you'll engage with this devotional in the way it was designed; savoring each contemplation one day at a time, and letting the ideas dwell in your heart and mind to take root there. The content builds from the opening, day by day, section by section, until the climax is eventually reached. And just as with other climaxes, rushing takes away from the pleasure and meaning of the process itself.

If you simply can't stand it and must read the whole thing in a heady rush, then I urge you to go back to the beginning after that. Experience the slow build. Savor each bite. Let God be with you and speak to you about their love and desire throughout the weeks it takes to reach completion.

I'm confident you'll be glad you did.

CREATOR AND CREATED

Our exploration of God's desire for us begins by reflecting on the Divine and our imaging of that divinity.

DAY 1:   GOD IS LOVE

*Beloved, let's love one another, for love is of God; and everyone who loves
has been born of God, and knows God. He who doesn't love doesn't know
God, for God is love.*
(1 John 4:7-8 WEB)

God is love.

My theology increasingly revolves around this key truth, the
various tenets of it held in motion by the force of its incredible mass.
This reality is as simple and pure as the phrase "I love you," but like
that phrase, it's rich with texture and nuance, and abundant in
variations of meaning. The concept can be endlessly contemplated,
and for the lucky, it can be experienced.

God is love.

All the forms of love, all the pain and promise of love, all the
comfort and nurture of love, all the calling to do better of love, all the
yearning and satisfaction of love.

God is Love itself, and because we are made in God's image, we
are by nature lovers. There is nothing more natural to us than loving.
If we reflect God's essence, we must also *be* love. Our time here and
now, with bodies made of spinning particles of energy, is a journey of
discovering what it means to *be* love, and to live fully into that reality
as Jesus did.

God is love, and we are love, called and drawn to seek deep union
with others and with God. The forces of darkness want to disrupt
and distort this reality in all sorts of ways, including our
understanding and use of sex. We were created as sexual beings in
part as a reflection of the Creator, which means sex is good and right
and even holy.

God is love.

I urge you to spend some time resting in this truth. Think about
what it means. Think about all the ways it might apply, especially
those ways you haven't considered before. Think about all the ways

you love, and how those ways might extrapolate out to the God in whose image and likeness we are formed.

God is love.

Love wants us to sample His goodness, with unlimited samplings.
Catherine Toon

DAY 2:   THE INTIMACY OF THE TRINITY

And above all these things put on love, which is the bond of perfectness.
(Colossians 3:14 ASV)

There are many theories about how the mystery of the Trinity works. Some say love is the connecting force which binds the three together. Others say the Trinity is a circle of never ending outpouring; an enclosed water wheel where one pours out and empties into the next, which pours out and empties into the third, which does the same back to the first.

A God who is Trinity tells us something about ourselves. The longing for each other which compels each person of the Three to be one with the next is the same force which creates in us a hunger to be one with another. The same seeking for union, for fullness, for completion by giving and receiving.

We are made in the image and likeness of God. Not just of the Creator, not just of Jesus who was also human, and not just of the Spirit. In the image of all three, we are made.

This reality doesn't mean we simply reflect the *characteristics* we associate with each of the persons. We are those things, yes. But we must also be made in the likeness of the bond which connects them, that force of love which knits not only the persons but the entire universe together. That same love acting like the pull of electrons toward the neutrons in atoms, or the gravitational force of planets circling the sun.

We image that electric hum desiring unity.

God created existence for reasons which defy our comprehension. Life fulfills some desire God has, and humans hold a particular role in that fulfillment. You would think the Trinity would be complete in itself, all fulfilling, all quenching, and yet God desires more.

God desires us.

In turn we also hunger for more, reaching for the completion which comes through another.

We could say, "In the beginning was the relationship" or the original blueprint for everything else that exists. John's word for that was Logos (John 1:1). In other words, the first blueprint for reality was relationality. It is all of one piece. Thus, we must read the whole Bible as a school of relationship.
Richard Rohr

DAY 3: MARY'S CONCEPTION OF JESUS

*Mary said to the angel, "How can this be, seeing I am a virgin?" The
angel answered her, "The Holy Spirit will come on you, and the power of
the Most High will overshadow you. Therefore also the holy one who is
born from you will be called the Son of God.*
(Luke 1:34-35 WEB)

Luke is the only gospel writer to capture this moment, and shortly
after these words, the account fades to black. But God has given us
the gift of imagination and invites us to populate the stories of
scripture with sound, scent, and texture. Here's what I envision:

Gabriel leaves. The Holy Spirit descends and God steps into time
and space, sweeping Mary into the scenes of the Song of Songs:

*How beautiful is your love, my sister, my bride!
How much better is your love than wine,
the fragrance of your perfumes than all kinds of spices!*
(Song of Songs 4:10 WEB)

Most Christians sanitize this encounter, stripping it of the gorgeous
sensuality it promises, as if a non-physical implantation of Jesus'
being is somehow holier than Mary being ravished by the Holy Spirit.
But Jesus is like us in all ways. His humanity was physical, borne by
Mary, born from the union of two.

Why doesn't this story confirm the sacredness of physical intimacy,
rather than demanding that none took place? God could have chosen
to present Jesus some other way, say, by molding him from the muck
like Adam, or poofing him into being fully formed, or replicating him
from an idea like the multiplication of a loaf and some fishes?
Instead, we are presented with a fully human God, begotten through
union with a woman. Jesus was implanted, became a zygote, and
developed into a baby whose birth we celebrate each December. We
accept the rawness of the infant Jesus lying in a feeding trough, but
reject the idea that his coming into being could have included
passion.

Isn't it more like a God of love to engulf Mary fully, satisfyingly,
even mind-blowingly rather than engaging in some kind of spiritual

6

artificial insemination? Is God more like the handsome lover described in the Song of Songs—comely and eager to rejoin the beloved—or like a lab technician wearing rubber gloves and a face mask, striving to retain as much distance as possible while performing an action of great intimacy?

If you present this idea to most Christians, they cringe and say that it couldn't have been a lush, physical encounter for Mary because it isn't described that way in the Bible. But the only way Luke would know what happened was through God's whispers and Mary's retelling of the story. And not many of us share the intimate details of our lovemaking.

We shouldn't find it surprising that Luke's story fades to black. The mother of God treasured *many* things in her heart.

> *God is not ashamed of the lowliness of human beings. God marches right in. He chooses people as his instruments and performs his wonders where one would least expect them.*
> Dietrich Bonhoeffer

DAY 4: BIG BANG INDEED

And God said, Let there be light. And there was light.
(Genesis 1:3 DARBY)

Christian cosmology establishes this statement as the singularity through which all energy, matter, time, and space came into being. It initiated everything which followed, right down to the inevitability of humanity and even you and I here together, pondering these thoughts.

Can you imagine God's "Let there be light" as anything short of cataclysmically explosive?

All of creation reflects God's being, with humans most like them. In human lovemaking, there is an intensification of love, and of passion, pleasure, and joy, which eventually culminates in a great unleashing of force.

Given that we are made in God's image and likeness, I imagine such a buildup within them as they prepared to burst forth with all of creation. I imagine God's love, passion, pleasure, and joy reaching such a fever pitch that it exploded, creating matter, energy, light, time, and space. All of this taking place within a covenant of love; the love between the Trinity, the love between God and us, the love that is the force of every molecular bond which holds matter together.

Big Bang indeed.

Yesterday we explored what Mary experienced when the Son of God was implanted by the Holy Spirit. Today we imagine what it was like for our great and glorious God to become begotten.

What was God's experience when they said for the second time "Let there be light" so that the light of the world would come into existence? Did they with the entire universe shudder in a great paroxysm of exultation and wonder, a second bang of eternity-rattling consequence?

Through procreation, we are co-creators of souls with God. That's not to say that the sole purpose of sex is to create new beings. But consider the beautiful reality that built in to our design is the innate ability to do what God did and does: make people. And people are not just the beings who roam around the world, building cathedrals, writing books, and getting up to all kinds of trouble. People are new souls which will exist eternally. This is an extraordinary gift and responsibility.

No wonder the forces of darkness work so hard to corrupt sexuality. It is the very power of God.

The whole difference between a construction and a creation is exactly this: that a thing constructed can be loved after it is constructed; but a thing created is loved before it exists.
G.K. Chesterton

DAY 5: MADE IN THE IMAGE AND LIKENESS OF GOD

So God created man in his own image, in the image of God created he him; male and female created he them.
(Genesis 1:27 KJV)

This statement resounds with meaning. It's like a prism, taking the fullness of light and offering up a wondrous array of color.

One of the many meanings to be contemplated is that we are not *merely* creatures; we are made in the image and likeness of God. This tells us something about ourselves, but it also tells us something about God. The Creator brought into being a world full of scents and tastes and textures, and created us to be highly sensory beings; so focused on sound that we become musicians, so focused on sights that we become visual artists, so focused on movement that we become dancers, so focused on taste and touch that we sometimes become gluttons or obsessive seekers of sex.

So let's talk about sex. Sex is an intrinsic part of humanity. It must somehow also then be an intrinsic part of divinity, though differently.

For humans, the sexual act is (optimally) characterized by intense pleasure, which settles into a slower, longer lasting contentment. When we don't engage in sexual activity many people feel bottled up, frustrated, and out of sorts. So what does this say about God in whose image we are made?

God must also be frustrated when their creative bursting force is damped down by our refusal to accept the love they extend. But God would never force our *yes*. They want us, simply, to desire them just as much as they desire us.

The world is created as a means of God's self-revelation so that, like a mirror or footprint, it might lead us to love and praise the Creator. We are created to read the book of creation so that we may know the Author of Life. This book of creation is an expression of who God is and is meant to lead humans to what it signifies, namely, the eternal Trinity of dynamic, self-diffusive love.
Sister Ilia Delio

10

DAY 6: GOD LOVES BODIES

And the Word became flesh, and dwelt among us (and we have contemplated his glory, a glory as of an only-begotten with a father), full of grace and truth; (John bears witness of him, and he has cried, saying, This was he of whom I said, He that comes after me is preferred before me, for he was before me;) for of his fulness we all have received, and grace upon grace. For the law was given by Moses: grace and truth subsists through Jesus Christ.
(John 1:14-17 DARBY)

The scriptures are saturated with sensory descriptions. The Song of Songs is filled with the taste of figs and the scent of myrrh sachets. The sights and smells of the temple are lavishly detailed: the sheen of precious metals; the odors of specially mixed incense, smoke, and blood; the silkiness of curtains; the taste of bread. There are darker descriptions as well of course, when the organs of sacrificed animals are consumed on the altar, and when fish die and rot because the Nile is turned to blood. But creation begins with the singing of the stars, and blossoms into a verdant garden.

The Bible offers scene after scene of food and feasting, of dance and song, of childbirth and physicality. And the culmination of it all is the incarnation of Jesus, when the Word became flesh.

God loves bodies. They love your body and their own. They created a world full of bodily creatures who come together to participate in creation. They love the intermingling of bodies in love, and the pleasure which results. God loves bodies in all their ache and need, so much so that they begat themself to experience it directly.

Don't be afraid of your bodily desires and the pleasure of your senses. They were designed by God, understood by God, and experienced by God.

The Word became *flesh*, after all.

Through its longing for Christ, whom it desires to breathe in as the Word inviting us to the enjoyment of full union, it receives a spiritual sense of smell, so that it may walk in the fragrance of Christ's ointments: and thus Christ is its life. And finally, through the love which binds it to Christ the incarnate Word, it receives straight from him, even during this earthly pilgrimage, a sense of taste which enables it to taste how sweet the Lord is. And by embracing him in that pure love which transforms its very being, it receives a spiritual sense of touch.

Polanco, a disciple of Ignatius

Day 7: The Woman Who Inspired Jesus to Wash Feet

Behold, a woman in the city who was a sinner, when she knew that he was reclining in the Pharisee's house, brought an alabaster jar of ointment. Standing behind at his feet weeping, she began to wet his feet with her tears, and she wiped them with the hair of her head, kissed his feet, and anointed them with the ointment.
(Luke 7:37-38 WEB)

Take a minute to imagine this scene. Smell the scents of supper, men, and lamp oil as you enter the room. See the flickering light reflected on the skeptical faces of the Pharisees reclined around the table. Find the soft gaze of Jesus at his own place, welcoming you to come closer. Feel your heart leap at his invitation, and the gut-wrenching guilt of all the ways you've screwed up.

Enter into the experience of being that woman, so overcome by joy and grief that she wept, seeing the dirt on Christ's feet, knowing he should have been attended to, and using her tears and hair to clean them. Pouring out expensive perfume to honor them, to soothe them, perhaps to comfort him and give him pleasure.

This is a picture of intense intimacy. It's the most physical encounter with the God-Man Jesus described in the scriptures. And Jesus permitted it. Not only that, he lauded it, and held her up as a model for the kind of actions his hosts should have taken.

After this, Jesus goes on to wash the feet of his apostles at the last supper, imitating the action of love she'd shown. Scripture doesn't report it, but I wonder if he did as she had done; kissing their feet which were damp with water and tears.

God longs for this kind of relationship with us; a mutual give and take of care and attention. They long for your heart to ache to touch and experience them with this kind of deep intimacy.

We are this woman, or we can be, acting like God, for God. Desiring to serve and love, to be served and be loved.

Truth isn't always beauty, but the hunger for it is.
Nadine Gordimer

Day 8: Immanuel in the Bedroom

Behold, the virgin shall be with child, and shall bring forth a son,
And they shall call his name Immanuel; which is, being interpreted, God
with us.
(Matthew 1:23 ASV)

Many Christians have a deistic understanding of God, in which the Creator breathed the universe into being and then stepped away to watch what would happen. In this view, God is separate from us and often disapproving. While most Christians believe in the power of prayer—requiring that God have *some* level of ongoing involvement—there's still an essential separateness between humanity and divinity.

When we view God this way, we ignore the scriptures which say we are temples of the Spirit; holy dwelling places for God. We have trouble accepting that *we are* the body of Christ, and also his friend, and his bride. There is deep intimacy in each of these relational descriptors which connects to the truth Matthew captured in today's scripture:

God is with us.

This isn't merely a description of the incarnation, and it's not a past state. Jesus was, and is, and is to come. He is the Alpha and the Omega, the once and always. God is around you, and within you.

The God-human Jesus is named Immanuel so we can reject a notion of distance and instead recall God's constant presence. In every touch and whisper, in every moment of passion, God is there.

Don't let this disturb you. There's no need for embarrassment or shame whether you are in a boardroom, a barroom, or a bedroom.

God is with you.

God is holding you to the earth with the force of gravity, pushing up and out from your very heart, and hovering above you as you sleep. God is with you, adores you, and takes great pleasure in you. God is in every ounce of blood coursing through your veins, every living and dying cell as your body ages, and every pulsing pleasure you receive through orgasm.

God is with you. Immanuel is there.

It happens sometimes that the Lord himself moves our souls and forces us, as it were, to this or that particular action by laying our souls wide open. This means that he begins to speak in the very depths of our being, without any clamour of words, he enraptures the soul completely into his love and bestows upon us an awareness of himself so that, even if we wished, we should be unable to resist.

St. Ignatius

LONGING

Now that we've grounded our contemplation in the reality of God as love, and humans as a manifestation of God, we move on to the experience of longing.

The sensation of yearning is universal to humanity. We long for many things; home, the past, a loved one, a future. In this section we explore longing to consider what it means for us and for God.

DAY 9: HOLY ADVENTING

For I consider that the sufferings of this present time are not worthy to be compared with the glory which will be revealed toward us. For the creation waits with eager expectation for the children of God to be revealed. For the creation was subjected to vanity, not of its own will, but because of him who subjected it, in hope that the creation itself also will be delivered from the bondage of decay into the liberty of the glory of the children of God. For we know that the whole creation groans and travails in pain together until now. Not only so, but ourselves also, who have the first fruits of the Spirit, even we ourselves groan within ourselves, waiting for adoption, the redemption of our body. For we were saved in hope, but hope that is seen is not hope. For who hopes for that which he sees? But if we hope for that which we don't see, we wait for it with patience.

In the same way, the Spirit also helps our weaknesses, for we don't know how to pray as we ought. But the Spirit himself makes intercession for us with groanings which can't be uttered. He who searches the hearts knows what is on the Spirit's mind, because he makes intercession for the saints according to God.
(Romans 8:18-27 WEB)

Today's passage speaks about creation's expectant yearning for what is to come. It talks about the pain of being subject to the reality of this world, which includes feelings of disconnectedness, discouragement, and pain. We often feel isolated and sometimes even downright hopeless.

This is one of the reasons the season of Advent is so important. It reminds us of what is to come, and *who* is to come. No wonder we push Christmas earlier and earlier each year, putting out red and green decorations right after Halloween, giving a token nod to Thanksgiving and forgetting the importance of the purple season of waiting. We are desperate for the Christ to come, desperate for the one who arrives as a baby but who grows to embrace us, to touch our blindness and deafness, to stem our bleeding, to wash our feet and feed us breakfast when we are cold and discouraged.

Our spirits groan while we wait.

But we are not alone.

The Spirit groans not only for us, but with us. God longs for the future which can and will be, and even now is; even more than we do.

In Luke 12 Jesus tells us he came to set the earth on fire, and wishes it were already burning. He longed for the culmination of his mission to oneness then, and still longs for it.

The God we long for has come, and is coming, and will always come; a Holy, perpetual adventing.

> *Batter my heart, three-person'd God, for you*
> *As yet but knock, breathe, shine, and seek to mend;*
> *That I may rise and stand, o'erthrow me, and bend*
> *Your force to break, blow, burn, and make me new.*
> *I, like an usurped town to another due,*
> *Labor to admit you, but oh, to no end;*
> *Reason, your viceroy in me, me should defend,*
> *But is captived, and proves weak or untrue.*
> *Yet dearly I love you, and would be loved fain,*
> *But am betrothed unto your enemy;*
> *Divorce me, untie or break that knot again,*
> *Take me to you, imprison me, for I,*
> *Except you enthrall me, never shall be free,*
> *Nor ever chaste, except you ravish me.*
>
> John Donne

DAY 10: THE SOUL'S THIRST

O God, Thou art my God, earnestly do I seek Thee,
Thirsted for Thee hath my soul,
Longed for Thee hath my flesh,
In a land dry and weary, without waters. (Psalm 63:1 YLT)

As a hart doth pant for streams of water,
So my soul panteth toward Thee, O God.
My soul thirsted for God,
for the living God,
When do I enter and see the face of God?
(Psalm 42:1, 2 YLT)

Most of Western society has easy access to water. We simply walk to a tap and turn it on. Not only that, the water is generally of very high quality; clean and pure.

But for much of the world, drought is a serious issue. Access to water was a recurring problem during the years the Psalms were written, and still is today. The scriptures show that miraculous springs of water were given to God's people and promised in the glorious eternity which is to come.

You may not have experienced true water scarcity, but you've been thirsty, right? Take a moment to recall a time when you ate too much salt, or spent a long time in the sun, or worked out without remembering to hydrate. Feel the sensation of need which rises up. Now imagine not having a drink to quench it.

Does this sensation line up with anything you feel emotionally? Can you compare that depth of physical sensation to an experience of the heart?

Our hearts are left parched by the pains of the world, hurts inflicted by ourselves, our loved ones, or by chance. Our souls are restless and search to be filled, and quenched.

I once had a dream in which I hammered a nail into the granite wall of a building being transformed into a church. Out of the hole sprung a stream of miraculous water; thicker than the water we know, and containing some sparkling element like magical glitter. I was astonished and filled with joy, as if this outpouring was a sign of favor to come.

The water God promises to quench our unending thirst is more glorious than we can envision, even at our thirstiest.

If your soul is currently panting like a deer who has wandered far in a drought, searching for a drink, imagine the quenching that is to come. The living water will transform your being in ways you aren't capable of envisioning.

The thirst you feel means that satisfaction is coming.

The sea does not reward those who are too anxious, too greedy, or too impatient. To dig for treasures shows not only impatience and greed, but lack of faith. Patience, patience, patience is what the sea teaches. Patience and faith. One should lie empty, open, choiceless as a beach—waiting for a gift from the sea.
Anne Morrow Lindbergh

DAY 11: THE PAIN OF DENIAL

I adjure you, O daughters of Jerusalem,
if you find my beloved,
that you tell him that I languish with love.
(Song of Songs 5:8 DRA)

Love is often messy and complicated. Sometimes we fall in love with a person who doesn't love us back. Sometimes we love someone who can't be in relationship with us.

There is suffering in these situations of self-denial. There is the pain of restrained love; pain in wanting to unleash love and comfort and giving and sharing but having to stop. Having to hold back out of a greater love, and a greater desire for the best of the beloved.

I think this kind of pain reflects God's experience of loving us. They could lavish us if they desired, unleashing love so magnificently that it would remove our ability to *choose* to love them back, because in our ravishment, there would only be *YES*. Instead, God gives us the opportunity to reach for them out of our own love.

Allow your heart to go there for a minute. Think about what union with your creator would feel like, in your body and your spirit. Consider how your very atoms would respond. And then pull back, and feel the loss. Experience the distance.

When we can't consummate the love we feel for another human, we mimic our God who also denies themself consummation.

Our aching will be fulfilled at the moment our bodies give up life. But God will continue to ache in their desire to consummate with all creation, throughout the eons.

The whole life of the good Christian is a holy longing. What you desire ardently, as yet you do not see... by withholding of the vision, God extends the longing, through longing he extends the soul, by extending he makes room in it. Let us long because we are to be filled... that is our life, to be exercised by longing.
St. Augustine

DAY 12: WANTING AS PART OF HAVING

But if we hope for that which we see not, we wait for it with patience.
(Romans 8:25 DRA)

There was a period in my life when I was desperately unhappy and wanted all of it to end so I could join with the eternal and be done with the struggle. During this time I was gifted with an intense longing and hunger for God. When this happened my heart felt like it was burning, and my chest ached with an emptiness yearning to be filled. The pain was intense, but as it continued, the love and longing morphed into what felt like an experience of God, a realization of them. Perhaps even a manifestation of them.

C.S. Lewis said:

The very nature of Joy makes nonsense of our common distinction between having and wanting.

The wanting of God I experienced so intensely was in fact a way of touching them.

Think about it this way: remember how it feels when you *really* want a big pile of French fries or that first cup of coffee in the morning? You imagine the crunch and salt of potato, the whoosh of caffeine after a few sips from your mug. You want these things because you are already perceiving their characteristics. You experience them in small part, and want more.

Anticipation is part of the experience in the same way Christmas Eve is exciting because of the joy of the next day.

It's hard to apply this to deep longings of the soul, especially when the longing connects to a loss. But our desire for union is a way of anticipating the fullness of what is to come.

A way, even, of *experiencing* what is to come.

Your heart may hurt and yearn for many things. But in this yearning you can taste and see the goodness of God who waits *with* you, to be reunited.

> *The holy is hungry for us and through us. And when we embody love in the world it is our minds and souls and our bodies that hunger. And when we live love, it is not just by feeding the poor or healing the sick—it is also by wanting and longing, it is by finding pleasure and taking delight in the world.*
>
> Rev. Molly Housh Gordon

DAY 13: THE BLOSSOMING OF DESIRE

Not that I have already obtained, or am already made perfect; but I press
on, that I may take hold of that for which also I was taken hold of by
Christ Jesus. I press on toward the goal for the prize of the high calling of
God in Christ Jesus.
(Philippians 3:12, 14 WEB)

Have you ever wondered what will happen to our desires when we leave this world; desires which are often tarnished with a patina of selfishness?

My first thought was that they will burn away like dross as our metal is purified. But that is too simple, and too dismissive of beauty.

Then I wondered if these desires might be fuel for the burning fire of love for God; the beatific vision enrapturing them in its raging core of flame. Rather than simply burning away, they will feed the fire that keeps the Trinity united, and grow it.

This explanation was better, but still didn't ring quite true.

I finally concluded that the desires we carry will blossom and bloom after death. Instead of being removed or subsumed, they will expand and grow until our whole being burns with love and desire and passion for all of creation, rather than for little pieces of it. Just as God's being does.

The mysteries of love and desire are worthy objects of our contemplation, though their realities must be much larger and more magnificent than anything we can imagine.

I can't wait to experience the truth. Press on, my fellow traveler, and you'll find out too.

O hearts, let not your many griefs
Distress you! You shall soon blossom;
You shall row through all storms,
Until you come to that luxuriant land
Where Beloved and loved one shall wholly flow through each other…
Hadewijch

DAY 14: LOVE SEEKS UNION

Set me as a seal upon thy heart,
As a seal upon thine arm:
For love is strong as death;
Jealousy is cruel as Sheol;
The flashes thereof are flashes of fire,
A very flame of Jehovah.
Many waters cannot quench love,
Neither can floods drown it.
(Song of Songs 8:6, 7 ASV)

Sometimes love rages like a fire. This is especially true for romantic love, which is characterized by an intense desire for union with the beloved. That kind of yawning need is a search for completion, for wholeness, and is a reflection and continuation of our need for union with God.

Years ago I felt an ardent attraction to someone which would never be consummated. I thought yearning for another human that intensely was a bad thing, because I recognized that at least part of it was my misdirected hunger for the divine. But as I thought further I realized I was wrong about it being bad. God gives us a desire for completion with and through other humans because each of us is a reflection of God, and a carrier of God. When we become one with another in a healthy, mutually giving way, we are in fact a more complete reflection of God's fullness, though still incomplete.

In romantic love, the two become one as we will eventually become one with God. Our feelings of romantic love and longing are dim views of what is to come. Even when those feelings are directed at someone with whom we will never connect.

We now see as through a glass darkly. Just imagine what it will be like when the veil is removed, and we see face to face.

We want something else which can hardly be put into words—to be united
with the beauty we see, to pass into it, to receive it into ourselves, to bathe
in it, to become part of it.
C.S. Lewis

26

Day 15:   The Woman at the Well

A woman of Samaria came to draw water. Jesus said to her, "Give me a drink." For his disciples had gone away into the city to buy food. The Samaritan woman therefore said to him, "How is it that you, being a Jew, ask for a drink from me, a Samaritan woman?" (For Jews have no dealings with Samaritans.) Jesus answered her, "If you knew the gift of God, and who it is who says to you, 'Give me a drink,' you would have asked him, and he would have given you living water. The woman said to him, "Sir, you have nothing to draw with, and the well is deep. So where do you get that living water? Are you greater than our father, Jacob, who gave us the well and drank from it himself, as did his children and his livestock?" Jesus answered her, "Everyone who drinks of this water will thirst again, but whoever drinks of the water that I will give him will never thirst again; but the water that I will give him will become in him a well of water springing up to eternal life." The woman said to him, "Sir, give me this water, so that I don't get thirsty, neither come all the way here to draw."
(John 4:7-15 WEB)

A Lutheran pastor friend tweeted a contemporized interpretation of this exchange, presenting Jesus as a dude in a bar, flirting with the Samaritan woman. It was a steamy interpretation, because my friend gave unfamiliar (to me) prominence to the erotic symbolism of thirst, gushing waters, and deep wells. Apparently her view is not singular; many scholars have read sensual overtones in the story.

Thirst is a powerful sensation. It signals a critical human need, because without water, we die. You can live without food for about three weeks. You can only survive without water for about three days.

And so we encounter this tale of mutual thirst. A God-man tired from his mission, tired from walking, tired of humanity's disinterest, arrives thirsty. Thirsting for water. Thirsting for response. Then along comes this woman, carrying her water jug in the heat of the day, planning merely to fill it as she always does and bear it back home for use in countless mundane ways. Jesus sees her and recognizes something. Perhaps it was in her eyes, or maybe the twitch of her hip, or deep in her heart. Maybe it was all three. He recognizes her hunger, and understands it as a reflection of his own. And so begins a

27

verbal dance; the longest recorded one-on-one conversation Jesus has in the gospels. A conversation in which he and the woman speak of filling and being filled, in which he asks to please be quenched.

Jesus mentions being thirsty one other time; on the cross, when he thirsts for it all to be over, for the culmination to take place. He was thirsty from carrying the instrument of his torture through town and up the incline to Golgatha, thirsty from hanging on the cross as the hours passed, thirsty from humanity's ceaseless refusal to accept love.

The encounter with the woman whose husband was no real husband was a precursor of that thirst, without the agony, and a hint of what will ultimately come.

She said yes to the filling he offered and raced away to tell the world about this miraculous lover.

He stayed behind, watching over the water jar she'd abandoned in her ecstasy, smiling, and feeling sated by her response. His thirst quenched for the moment, without having received any of the water she'd come to draw. Quenched by her yes.

Our God still thirsts as Jesus did that day, for that woman and for all of us. God thirsts for you, right now.

Close your eyes, and feel their thirst.

The sea hath bounds, but deep desire hath none.
William Shakespeare

DAY 16: THAT THEY MAY BE ONE

*And I do not demand for these only, but also for those who believe on me
through their word; that they may be all one, as thou, Father, art in me,
and I in thee, that they also may be one in us, that the world may believe
that thou hast sent me. And the glory which thou hast given me I have
given them, that they may be one, as we are one; I in them and thou in me,
that they may be perfected into one and that the world may know that thou
hast sent me, and that thou hast loved them as thou hast loved me.
Father, as to those whom thou hast given me, I desire that where I am they
also may be with me, that they may behold my glory which thou hast given
me, for thou lovedst me before the foundation of the world. Righteous
Father,—and the world has not known thee, but I have known thee, and
these have known that thou hast sent me. And I have made known to
them thy name, and will make it known; that the love with which thou
hast loved me may be in them and I in them.*
(John 17:20-26 DARBY)

This passage has pulled at my heart for years. It reads like poetry,
with its circling call to become one, with us and them, together
mystically but also actually. It is gorgeous, puzzling poetry which
speaks of God's desire for us to be unified with each other and in
union with God.

The longing of Jesus' heart rings loud. Do you recall what it's like
when you are really excited about something, or feel strongly but
don't know how to say what you mean? The words come gushing
out, sometimes confusedly, sometimes profoundly, all in a jumble.
You might even repeat yourself because you're so worked up. That
seems to be what's happening in this passage. It takes place
immediately before John's description of Judas' betrayal in that dark
garden. Jesus knows time is short, and this message of union is
critical. And so his words pour out with passion.

God longs for our oneness. They yearn for us to be as closely knit
as the Trinity is, with no separation between unique persons, all of us
merging in love, embodying love, being filled with love. That we may
be one, as Jesus and the Creator are one; Jesus in us and the Creator
in him.

This is the mystical union to come.

Now, however, I think we need less catechesis and more profound mystagogia…. Mystagogia deals less with teaching but rather unfolds the symbols of our celebration in a more poetic mode, gradually forming the deeper affections of our heart.
Dennis Chester Smolarski

MYSTICAL MARRIAGE, HOLY CONSUMMATION, AND THE ECSTASY TO COME

The word "consummation" is full of meaning and connotation. It comes from two root terms: "con," meaning "altogether" and "summa," meaning "sum total" or "highest, supreme." When you put the two terms together the meaning is "the highest level of being together."

Perhaps more interestingly, the term hides within it the word "consume," which in a Christian context is quite important.

Read on to contemplate why.

DAY 17: THE WEDDING AT CANA

*And on the third day a marriage took place in Cana of Galilee, and the
mother of Jesus was there. And Jesus also, and his disciples, were invited
to the marriage. And wine being deficient, the mother of Jesus says to him,
They have no wine. Jesus says to her, What have I to do with thee,
woman? mine hour has not yet come. His mother says to the servants,
Whatever he may say to you, do.*
(John 2:1-5 DARBY)

The idea of marital union is central to the scriptural image of God's
desire for us. Wedding imagery saturates the Bible from beginning to
end. We shouldn't be surprised then that the earliest miraculous action
of Jesus presented in the gospels would take place at a wedding
celebration.

In the cultural context of the day, marriage was a two-part process.
First came the contractual aspect of the betrothal, then came the
taking of the woman into the home of her husband. In between was
a period of waiting and anticipation. During this period, the couple is
together, yet apart, sometimes for up to a year.

Presumably, the wedding feast in this story celebrated the second
ceremony; the joining together of the couple's lives. The bride may
well have been carried by carriage from her father's home to the
groom's, to the wedding canopy: the chuppah.

The guests had already partied for so long that the wine ran out,
yet they still thirsted for celebration. They didn't want the wedding
feast to end. Meanwhile, the couple themselves *still* waited to become
fully one.

God shows up in this moment of prolonged anticipation, bringing
wine. And not just a little bit, but enough to fuel a party for a long
time. And not a box of the cheap grocery-store stuff, but top shelf.
Mary asked, and Jesus complied, producing great quantities of wine,
toasting the couple, toasting us, and toasting his own launch into a
ministry characterized by dramatic demonstrations of outrageous
love.

Our creator delights in their love for us, and our love for each other. Jesus feasts with us in anticipation of our eventual, mutual inebriation.

> *Wine enters through the mouth,*
> *Love, the eyes.*
> *I raise the glass to my mouth,*
> *I look at you,*
> *I sigh.*
> William Butler Yeats

DAY 18: MYSTICAL MARRIAGE

Let us rejoice and be exceeding glad, and let us give the glory unto him: for the marriage of the Lamb is come, and his wife hath made herself ready. And it was given unto her that she should array herself in fine linen, bright and pure: for the fine linen is the righteous acts of the saints.

And he saith unto me, Write, Blessed are they that are bidden to the marriage supper of the Lamb. And he saith unto me, These are true words of God.
(Revelation 19:7-9 ASV)

Today we explore an idea which has been a theme from the very beginning of Christianity; that God desires a relationship with us based on marital oneness rather than subordination and obedience. It's a key subject, so we're going to take a bit of extra time on it.

Christians from ancient days until now have looked to those who came before us as a great crowd of witnesses who can offer insight into what it means to be a follower of God. Many of these siblings in Christ can be described as Christian mystics, meaning they sought by contemplation and self-surrender to obtain unity with God, and by doing so, experienced God in ways which transcend the intellect. Some of these encounters sound quite sexual. Here are a few examples:

An Italian Dominican nun from the 14th century named Catherine of Siena wrote letters about her mystical marriage with Christ. Her experiences influenced her theology and her writings, such as this excerpt:

This I have told thee, my sweetest daughter, that thou mightiest know the perfection of this unitive state, when the eye of the intellect is ravished by the fire of My charity, in which charity it receives the supernatural light. With this light the souls in the unitive state love Me, because love follows the intellect, and the more it knows the more can't it love. Thus the one feeds the other, and, with this light, they both arrive at the Eternal Vision of Me, where they see and taste Me, in Truth, the soul being separated from the body, as I told thee when I spoke to thee of the blissfulness that the soul received in Me. This state is most excellent, when the soul, being yet in the mortal body, tastes bliss with the immortals, and ofttimes she arrives at so great a union that she scarcely knows whether she be in the body or out of it; and tastes the earnest-money of Eternal Life, both because she is united with Me, and because her will is dead in Christ, by which death her union was made with Me, and in no other way could she perfectly have done so.

John of the Cross was a Spanish mystic born in 1542, who served as a priest and a Carmelite friar. He wrote a poem called *Song of the Soul and the Bridegroom* which includes the following stanzas:

There He gave me His breasts,
There He taught me the science full of sweetness.
And there I gave to Him
Myself without reserve;
There I promised to be His bride.
My soul is occupied,
And all my substance in His service;
Now I guard no flock,
Nor have I any other employment:
My sole occupation is love.
If, then, on the common land
I am no longer seen or found,
You will say that I am lost;
That, being enamored,
I lost myself; and yet was found.

Teresa of Ávila was a Spanish theologian nun born in 1515 and a contemporary of John of the Cross who had a vision of an angel from God. Here's how she described the encounter:

I saw in his hand a long spear of gold, and at the iron's point there seemed to be a little fire. He appeared to me to be thrusting it at times into my heart and to pierce my very entrails; when he drew it out, he seemed to draw them out also, and to leave me all on fire with a great love of God. The pain was so great, that it made me moan; and yet so surpassing was the sweetness of this excessive pain, that I could not wish to be rid of it. The soul is satisfied now with nothing less than God. The pain is not bodily, but spiritual; though the body has its share in it, even a large one. It is a caressing of love so sweet which now takes place between the soul and God, that I pray God of His goodness to make him experience it who may think that I am lying.

35

These experiences may seem alien to your own faith walk. They aren't a requirement for Christian life, of course, but they don't have to be limited to the saints of the past. They still take place, and could even happen to you.

Mystical encounters of becoming the spouse of Christ have the power to transform your heart, your faith, and your work.

God wants to ravish us. Do you want to be ravished?

> *O hearts, let not your many griefs*
> *Distress you! You shall soon blossom;*
> *You shall row through all storms,*
> *Until you come to that luxuriant land*
> *Where Beloved and loved one shall wholly flow through each other...*
> Hadewijch

Day 19: The Two Become One

And the two shall become one flesh: so that they are no more two, but one flesh.
(Mark 10:8 ASV)

The theme of marital union with Jesus is stressed from Genesis through Revelation, when John speaks to us of the marriage feast we will celebrate when the final trumpet sounds. As the books of the Bible unfold, we hear about fidelity and infidelity, and the shining bride who is prepared for her bridegroom.

The church assigned so much importance to wedding imagery that Christian rituals still reflect it. In some denominations, babies wear long, white Christening gowns reminiscent of wedding dresses. In Roman Catholic tradition, girls receiving first communion wear frilly white dresses with similar connotations. In some religious orders, nuns don actual wedding gowns as part of their progression from postulant to making perpetual vows.

The idea of espousement with God runs deep, and has immense power. Catherine of Siena wrote about how knowing God helps us know ourselves, which helps us know God. It is a circular unfolding, with the biblical sense of "knowing," when we become one with the Trinity.

The idea that we can have true union with God is called "theosis." When we achieve it, we somehow participate in God's divine nature. Scripture might describe this as being a temple of the Holy Spirit, as being Jesus' sibling, or even—as Psalm 82 proclaims—as being gods ourselves. But the oneness Jesus describes in today's passage about what happens in marriage has meaning which runs much deeper: our union with God can actually be a participation in God's divinity.

In the section on longing we talked about Jesus' gorgeous prayer in John 17, when he begs the Creator that you and I become one with the Trinity. In today's passage we see what becoming one looks like; the action of two bodies, merging as they liturgize their love into physical action.

For several days I've been preaching to you about marriage, but it's time to make a confession:

It's not really about the wedding.

It's about the wedding night.

> *Purity most often leads to pride or to despair, not to holiness. Because holiness is about union with, and purity is about separation from.*
> Nadia Bolz-Weber

DAY 20: GOD'S LOVE SONG

Let him kiss me with the kisses of his mouth;
for your love is better than wine.
Your oils have a pleasing fragrance.
Your name is oil poured out,
therefore the virgins love you.
Take me away with you.
Let's hurry.
(Song of Songs 1:2-4a WEB)

Throughout the ages, theologians have viewed the sensual intensity of the Song of Songs as an illustration of God's love for the church, but also for us uniquely, as individual souls. Here are some words from St. Bernard of Clairvaux:

Only the touch of the Spirit can inspire a song like this, and only personal experience can unfold its meaning. Let those who are versed in the mystery revel in it; let all others burn with desire to attain this experience rather than merely learn about it.

Bernard wants us to understand that knowing God is not merely a matter for the mind. Exploring the Song of Songs can help us attain the experience as he describes. The book is the very height of gospel wisdom; the good news that God views us as a lover, with tender compassion and desire for union.

Go back and read the opening passage again.

It's downright steamy!

The woman longs for her beloved's kisses. She is inebriated from the scent of him, drunk on the wine of his love. She begs to be taken away by the one she adores.

Let's read on, to the bridegrooms response:

My dove in the clefts of the rock,
in the hiding places of the mountainside,
let me see your face.
let me hear your voice;
for your voice is sweet and your face is lovely.
(Song of Songs 2:14 WEB)

Can you hear the longing in their voice? "Let me see your face… Let me hear your voice… Reveal yourself to me, for I desire you."

The passion continues:

My beloved is mine, and I am his.
He browses among the lilies.
Until the day is cool, and the shadows flee away,
turn, my beloved,
and be like a roe or a young deer on the mountains of Bether.
(Song of Songs 2:16-17 WEB)

Such a sense of culmination is presented; a lover's time and touch stretching for hours, his strength like a stag in contrast to her own soft scent of lilies.

It's gorgeous.

Many Christians dismiss the Song of Songs as mere theological frippery, but the intensity of physical union presented offers a captivating view of God for those who can cast away the unholy shame. Read it, and open yourself to experience the kind of love your Creator feels for you.

There need be no embarrassment about entering into this erotic love song of ask and answer. Instead, sing your own song to God of their belovedness, and your own.

The beauty of the female is the root of joy to the female as well as to the
male, and it is no accident that the goddess of love is older and stronger
then the god. To desire the desiring of her own beauty is the vanity of
Lilith, but to desire the enjoying of her beauty is the obedience of Eve, and
to both it is in the lover that the beloved tastes her own delightfulness.
C. S. Lewis

DAY 21: GOD OF CONSUMMATION (I)

He that eats my flesh and drinks my blood dwells in me and I in him.
(John 6:56 DARBY)

And as they did eat, Jesus took bread, and blessed, and brake it, and gave
to them, and said, Take, eat: this is my body.
(Mark 14:22 KJV)

The words in these passages institute an action which is repeated in churches all around the globe every day of the year; that moment when a minister or priest stands before the assembly and reminds us that on the night before his death, Jesus took bread and wine, declared them to be his body and blood, and instructed us to partake of him. Some Christians believe the very particles of flour and fermented grapes are transformed into the flesh and blood of God. Some believe that the bread and wine are there at the same time as the body and blood. Others believe the real presence of God is mysteriously contained without defining how. Still others view it as merely a symbol of remembrance and unity.

No matter what perspective you take, I invite you to step deeper for a moment into this central ritual of our faith. I want you to consider the celebration as it is described in Revelation, and understood by the church for centuries: as a participation of the wedding celebration between us and God.

Culmination of our marriage.

Consummation of the promised bond.

Jesus offers us his body, mystically present in the staff of life, mystically present in the cup of wine produced miraculously in abundance, transformed from the living water of his being into the best wine, pouring into us and joining with the bread so we can become one as the two who are wed are one and as he is one with the Creator and the Spirit.

Communion contains the word "union" in part because together we become one with the being who created us, feeds us, and adores us; the lover of our souls.

41

Each time we receive God through this tasting of bread and wine, body and blood, despite having turned away from God over and over again throughout the days, weeks, or months between reception, our wedding vows are renewed and we become once again the bride of Christ, and he our spouse.

Despite our many failings and our repeated betrayals, he comes to us. We receive him, and are received.

We become one flesh again, and celebrate the wedding feast.

My belief in the Eucharist is simple: without touch, God is a monologue, an idea, a philosophy; he must touch and be touched, the tongue on the flesh, and that touch is the result of monologues, the idea, the philosophies which led to faith; but in the instant of the touch there is no place for thinking, for talking; the silent touch affirms all that, and goes deeper...
Andre Dubus II

DAY 22: GOD OF CONSUMMATION (II)

This is my body, which is given for you.
(Luke 22:19b WEB)

Yesterday we reflected on the marital merging which occurs through communion, with a focus on *our* experience. Today we open our hearts to the idea of *God's* experience.

During the most formative years for my faith, I attended a church which centered each service around the sacrament as many denominations do. I spent hours studying the history and meaning of the practice, and fell in love with it. Each Sunday I strove to open myself to the experience, and to be fully present to it. One week during this timeframe I sat after receiving the Eucharist, savoring God's body merging with the precious blood in my mouth, and willing my taste buds to perceive beyond appearances.

As I sat focusing, it occurred to me that in entering my body, in becoming one with me, God experienced joy. Being received by me was a holy reunion. A holy completion.

God's body and blood which had been separated by paten and chalice were reunited with each other and with the Spirit residing within me. God's body rejoined the body which is the church; a hypostatic reunion of the human and the divine.

It swept me off my feet, and to my knees.

It's still sweeping me now.

God invites you into this experience as well. They long to join you through feeding, through marital consummation, through their flesh becoming one with yours.

Your Creator, Comforter, and Savior longs to be one with you.

Say yes, and be fed.

Please remember there is a sexual nature to the Eucharist—"This is My Body, given up for you"—and we need to root that in human sexuality and in love, and it helps us to appreciate even better the Sacrament of the Eucharist.

Fr. Thomas Rosica

DAY 23: THE ECSTASY TO COME

Thou wilt show me the path of life:
In thy presence is fulness of joy;
In thy right hand there are pleasures for evermore.
(Psalm 16:11 ASV)

Our understanding of what will come after our days of enfleshment is veiled. The scriptures offer a few images of angelic hosts singing, gold-paved roads, and rivers whose verdant banks produce an abundance of fruit and miraculous healing. But the reality must be so much more intense, and unlike the world to which we are currently constrained.

Today's Psalm gives us a tiny foretaste; God's hand offers pleasures for eternity.

What might this mean?

We began this devotional by contemplating the being of God, and talking about the Big Bang of creation, when the Divine exploded matter into being. At the end of our understanding of time, when the energy of our souls disconnect from the matter of our bodies and we escape the constraints of time and space, I can't help but think we enter into that explosive energy of God's love, helping power the universe in its continual expansion, becoming truly one with the Three who are One, and experiencing the pleasure which comprises the hand of God as it sweeps across the expanse of nothingness to leave behind brand new stars and tiny new souls.

What will heaven be like?

45

We should expect nothing less than ecstasy.

> *It seems to me that when people say that they "talk with Jesus" or "feel Jesus in their hearts," they are referring in part to a very superficial level of the unconscious, which we would identify by a kind of warm nostalgia they associate with pleasant memories of their parents, probably quite distorted, or of the "good old days." This is not really the content of the unconscious at any level of depth. The feelings of the unconscious are more frequently identified with a sense of joy, as described by C.S. Lewis in his autobiography; a strange warmth, such as John Wesley testified to at Aldersgate; a celestial orgasm, as Teresa of Avila relates; a sublime melody, as the fourteenth-century mystic, Richard Rolle, claims; or the oceanic experience such as Castaneda himself records.*
> Urban T. Holmes III

DAY 24: UNSPEAKABLE JOY

Wherein you greatly rejoice, though now for a little while, if need be, you have been grieved in various trials, that the proof of your faith, which is more precious than gold that perishes even though it is tested by fire, may be found to result in praise, glory, and honor at the revelation of Jesus Christ—whom, not having known, you love. In him, though now you don't see him, yet believing, you rejoice greatly with joy that is unspeakable and full of glory.
(1 Peter 1:6-8 WEB)

Have you ever been so swept with wonder or joy that you're left speechless? Perhaps it happened at the birth of a child, or standing on the edge of the Grand Canyon, or looking at the sleeping face of your beloved. There are times when awe strikes so deep that words are too small to express what feels like an ocean of emotion.

I think this is what heaven will be like. We'll become one with all creation, engulfed in joy so profound that words can't suffice. Instead our beings will radiate with song. The tiny bits of energy which make up the universe will all vibrate with and from love, strumming and thrumming, wordless and matterless, alive with harmony.

You can experience it now, you know. Right now. Right where you sit, if it is quiet, and you can take a moment to enter in. It won't be like what is to come, of course. But you *can* experience it. The veil between what is and is to come is thin, and torn. The heaven that will be already is.

You can experience it now, if you sit a moment, and breathe deep, and imagine the molecules of your body each pulsing with the beat of God's heart, the rotation of the planets, and the expanding waves of the stars.

Our future with God will be filled with unspeakable joy.

It already is.

I have learnt to love you late, Beauty at once so ancient and so new! I have learnt to love you late! You were within me, and I was in the world outside myself. I searched for you outside myself and, disfigured as I was, I fell upon the lovely things of your creation. You were with me, but I was not with you. The beautiful things of this world kept me far from you and yet, if they had not been in you, they would have had no being at all. You called me; you cried aloud to me; you broke my barrier of deafness. You shone upon me; your radiance enveloped me; you put my blindness to flight; you shed your fragrance about me; I drew breath and now I grasp your sweet odour, I tasted you, and now I hunger and thirst for you. You touched me, and I am inflamed with love of your peace.
Augustine of Hippo

Conclusion

I once ate a peach and was transformed by the process. It was so juicy that it was more drinking than eating. The scent of it was like the perfume described in the Song of Songs.

Peaches can be magical in that way, when they are perfectly ripe.

We are all like that peach, full of magical possibility for delicious fulfillment. But there's a second half to the equation. The fullness of a fruit's existence isn't realized unless it is consumed. If it sits on the tree until it falls and then withers and rots, God's ingenious system kicks in so it will provide food for creatures and bacteria, fertilizing the soil, and maybe even growing into a new tree. But for the true magnificence of a peach to be realized, it must be eaten by a human, who can not only comprehend the beauty of its deliciousness, but can also wonder at its creation.

C.S. Lewis wrote:

It is in the lover that the beloved tastes her own delightfulness.

For our true magnificence to be realized, we must be consumed. We must offer up the exquisite uniqueness of ourselves to God, even to the point of complete ravishment. And having offered and received them in return, we must go out into the world and seek union with others, the circle of consummation and unity growing and expanding to fill the cosmos.

Allow yourself to desire.

Desire God as they desire you.

Consume God, and be consumed.

Embrace the reality of your spousal union with Christ, and change the world.

You are the Creator's perfect peach.

Made in the USA
Coppell, TX
25 July 2020